Cannon Golf Shot 3000
Power Golf Drive Distance Program

Cannon Golf Shot 3000
Power Golf Drive Distance Program

Chattanooga Bookmakers

Copyright © 2011 by Ronnie Helton

ISBN: Softcover 978-1-936912-22-3

All rights reserved. No part of this book may be reproduced or transmitted in any form or by any means, electronic or mechanical, including photocopying, recording, or by any information storage and retrieval system, without permission in writing from the publisher.

This book was printed in the United States of America.

To order additional copies of this book, contact:

Chattanooga Bookmakers
c/o Parson's Porch, Inc
1-423-475-7308
www.parsonsporch.com

Thanks

Mom

Michael, Jeffery, Johnny, and Ashleigh

Preface

You can't judge a book by its cover! Inside is the result of 40 years of study and practice with some of the best. It will work for you if you commit to it. I could have written a 200 page book and filled it full of stories, jokes, etc. but I chose to get down to the NITTY GRITTY and help you right away.

Ronnie Helton

Personal Agreement

I agree to myself to faithfully stick with this program.

I know it can be successful for me. It is a tried and true program with 40 years of success.

I will not give up without giving it a thorough try, even when the soreness kicks in. I won't fail unless I quit, and I won't quit.
I will be hitting Monster golf drive shots.

People will be amazed at me for hitting long drives.

I will be a great success!

_____   _____

Sign   Date

Now, copy this and post it up in places where you can always see it and let's get started!

(Disclaimer: This manual is sold for information only. The author is not responsible for any accidents. Check with your doctor before starting any training program. Use this method with great care.)

Dear Reader,

Thank you for purchasing this program. You must take your golf game seriously. Here in this program you won't find way for improving your or where to find the best clubs or gloves. This is a resistance training and drive technique for gold. With this method, it is possible to add 25-100 yards or even more to your drive. It is a tired and tested program that I developed over the last 40 years. People are amazed at how far I can het a golf ball.

I am a small man who has wrist speed on my side. I knew I had to develop something different to hang with the big boys.

People have asked me to offer theses methods for years, but I wanted to overcome the last obstacle - power.

So, now let's get to it. Start right now by signing the Personal Pledge, and it put it up where you can see it all the time.

Give yourself some time to get you muscles used to the method. No pain. No gain. Or, if little is our labor, little are our gains.

Ronnie Helton
2011

Exercise One
Weighted Swing

What happens when you take a strong rubber band and wind it up tighter and tighter and tighter, and then let go? A tremendous surge of energy meets anything in its path, especially if there is no resistance. What if you could adapt that force to your golf swing? Do you get my drift yet?

I want you to take an old golf club that you don't use anymore. If you can't spare one, I'll bet your local second-hand, or thrift shop has several to choose from. That is a further testament to all of the people who tried and failed at golf because they quit. Those people really don't understand the fierce competition on just about any level of golf. Everyone wants to win very badly for the bragging rights on the course and at the water cooler. Those people didn't have that extra advantage like you do now to be successful with your golf game.

Now you need to weigh down your golf club. I prefer a 1-pound or less weight to start with, that will attach to your club safely. You can also hold 2-3 clubs together. (See pictures below)

Now, let's loosen up those muscles. Grip the weighted club in both hands and carefully swing it round and round. Over, under, sideways, down. Move it across your back, and in every direction with both hands on the club. Do this for about 5 minutes, and then relax for a few minutes. After you've loosened up, do the same thing with just one hand at a time. We are trying to isolate and develop only muscles used for your swing.

You don't need to have the build of a football player for this to work. That is why we will only be dealing with those muscles in the actual golf swing. Stay on track with this light weight for a week or so, and then move up another half-pound. You build muscles as you increase the resistance. If you stayed at a light weight all the time your muscles would adjust and not increase in strength.

Swinging a slightly heavier driver club is like wearing weights on your feet and then taking them off. Your feet seem to jump off the ground!

Weighted Swing Exercises

Exercise 2: Ball Technique

Golf normally requires great exertion and speed to get the most distance from your swing. In baseball, you merely need to "meet the ball" because of the speed and force of the pitch. Hitting a fast moving baseball takes great skill but the distance comes without as much exertion. So, us golfers need every advantage to get those results.

I knew one of the greatest hitters of all time personally, and he told me to picture the bottom 1/3 of the ball in your mind's eye before you hit it. The key is to get the upspin on the ball for greater distance. Downspin does just the reverse. So, when you hit the golf ball too high on the tee, the uplift isn't as great. You want the air to also help you for distance because a ball spinning upward will get help from the air.

Mark a small "x" on the bottom 1/3 of your ball and concentrate on hitting that. There again, this

will take some steady practice. When you are not on the course, relax and simply picture yourself hitting that x on the ball. This technique of visualization for just a few moments, is equal to hours of practice time on the course. If you really want to improve your drive you must see it in your mind's eye first. Without vision, your dream will perish. I USE THIS TECHNIQUE ALL THE TIME. IT WORKS!

Exercise 3: Isometric Swing

This next exercise will give you some fantastic results. But, don't overdo this one. Take it easy and go very slow until you get the hang of it. I should tell you that you may need to wear brace for these exercises because of the strain on your wrists and fingers. If you are in any pain, stop for the day.

Lay your weighted club down and get another club that you don't use. You will damage this one if it has a metal shaft, I am sure. You may want to try fiberglass for this one but there is still no guarantee it won't break. Be careful!

I want you to stand in front of an unmovable object. A tree works well for this.

Now, stand erect as if you are getting ready to tee off Put the club up against the tree about tee height, and try to push it away from you. Exert all the force you can for about 10 seconds, then rest for 30 seconds and do it again. Do about 10 reps of these until you work your way up to 20 times per day. Don't overexert yourself! Go slow the first few times. (You may feel the need to reverse your grip and stance to the opposite side in order to balance out the muscles, that is fine for each of these isometric swing exercises.)

Place the club at the lowest point of your swing. Strain hard as if you were hitting a golf ball. Don't hit the pole. Just try to push it over. Hold for 10 seconds. Then two more times.

Second, put the club waist high and perform the same technique. Try to move that tree away from you. Again, push for 10 seconds, rest for 30, and do ten reps.

Finally, do the same exercise with the club totally outstretched as if at the end of your swing. Can you feel those swing muscles being worked?

Do these exercises regularly. At least five times per day while in training. You must feel some fatigue to get muscle swing strength.

Keeping Limber

I just wanted to say a few words about carpal tunnel syndrome and other hand and wrist problems. I am not a Dr., I can only tell you what worked for me. I played sports all of my life and keeping your hands and wrists moving with vigorous exercise is the key to keeping fluid from building up in your wrists and fingers. They can get so sore that you will want to rest them, but don't until you exercise them constantly. Bending your wrists back very gently is a good stretch to help you. Raise your hands high up and open and close your hands as fast as you can to keep your fingers loose and stress free. Garlic is good for blood circulation and general good health. Golfers stand and wait a lot on the course, so many experience bad circulation and joint problems. It would not be a crime to do simple stretching exercises while on the golf course.

Some people use wrist building devices to gain hand and wrist strength. Some people squeeze rubber balls and etc. but these exercises will not do enough for the swing muscles we are trying to super tone. That will require more rest for your hand and fingers. You won't need to use them. Take a good comfortably hot shower and focus the water on your swing muscles. There again, PLEASE DON'T OVERDO IT.

Swing Grip Technique

What is wrong with the picture below? It is the picture of an average swing grip. You can get some pretty good distance with this technique if you really swing hard and fast.

But what if you could streamline this swing grip even more? What if I could show you a grip that could allow you to absolutely crush a golf ball?

With most grips, too much resistance stops your wrists from breaking during the swing itself. Practice hand on hand in the usual way to swing. Quite a bit of drag, right? Well just hang on, I am about to show you my tried and proven technique to add extra distance to you swing. Let's look closer at the average grip.

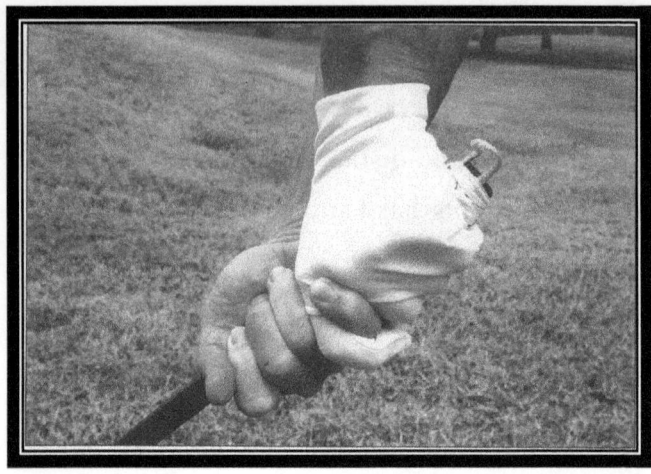

Too much hand on hand causes drag. Cramped up fingers cause friction to slow complete wrist speed follow through.

My Power Crushing System

I want you to start by using a driver that is about 1-2 inches shorter than you usually use. You will be adding an inch or so with this power stroke. I want you to take a piece of elastic waistband about 24 inches long. Have it sewn together so it will be 12 inches long. It needs to be $1/4$ inch wide. You can simply take the elastic out of a pair of underwear or buy some new elastic at your local hobby store or fabric store. The reason we use this is because of the grip of the rubber inside. (You can also use large rubber bands for this but they will need to be replaced often as the rubber tends to dry out.)

Now wrap it around the end of your golf driver tightly so it won't slip. Keep it all close to the edge. Don't let it get more than a Y2 inch width ball of elastic. This will be our club handle just like the handle of a baseball bat. This super grip feature will allow the club to pivot more forcefully before striking the ball. When you get it in your hand after tightly wrapping the elastic, let it rock back and forth in the tight grip. Can you feel the energy just waiting to be unleashed? It is like squeezing a firm rubber ball and releasing it very quickly.

Now place your hands and fingers just like shown in Figure 4B, C, D, & E on the next few pages. It will seem very awkward at first. Also, you need to wrap some elastic around your weighted club. Practice your new swing techniques with your weighted club. Take several swings for a couple of minutes. Now, pick up your converted driver. Doesn't it feel so much lighter and faster to swing? This will give you great club speed.

Important Safety Feature

Looped cord so club won't fly from hand—Before you put the elastic on your club, tape a loop of cord on the end underneath where the elastic will go with enough room for your pinkie finger to slip into. After you master the technique of using this loop, you can let the club pivot off the pinkie loop for increased distance. It works as a sort of slingshot.

Roll back and forth with one hand.

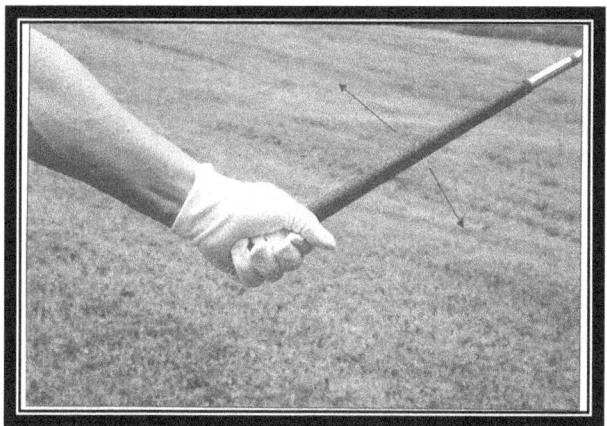

Ball of rubber elastic wrapped tightly bout ½ inch high.

Feel the ball of energy during this rocking motion. This is where extra force is applied to distance.

The 2 fingers above the pinkie allow the power pivoting motion. Squeeze tight. This is why you also swing the weighted club beforehand. The weighted club makes your fingers and wrists work harder so when you swing with your usual club, it will move just like coming out of a "cannon."

Pinkie finger must hang over the edge of the club, not underneath bottom of club.

If you are left handed, just simply reverse techniques.

The right hand goes against the bottom left hand tightly. The bottom 2 fingers of the top hand wrap around the top of the left or bottom hand.

Simply reverse techniques if you are left handed.

This swing technique allows for maximum wrist breaking action. The less of your wrists you use allows faster swing power.

BOTH HANDS

Swing your weighted club with this finger and wrist technique also.

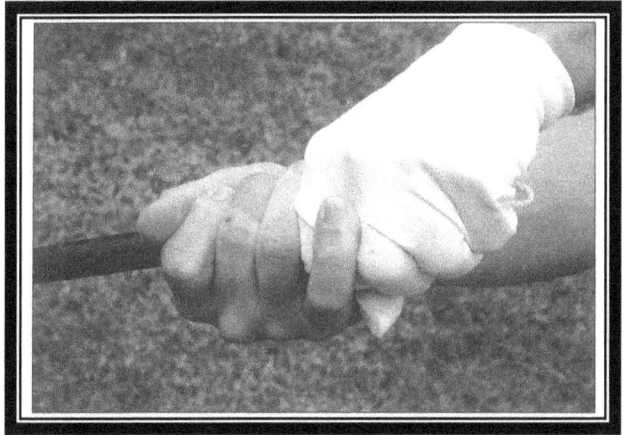

Keep bottom 2 fingers tight against left hand.

(When you swing your weighted club for 2 minutes before, this action will seem more natural.)

Your pinkie finger must hang over the end of the ball of elastic for swing control and super wrist breaking action. Again, grip the ball of elastic on the end of the club. Rock it back and forth. Can you feel the force? When you swing you get that force plus breakforce from your streamlined wrists. Now, notice I want you to place the ball on the tee 6 inches or so away from your left toe. This is to insure maximum striking force on the ball. When you hit the ball right down in front of you, you only get half of that force. In other words, you are almost into full body swing action. Your wrists and other swing muscles are extended. Study the pictures. It will seem extremely awkward at first but after a few days of practice it will seem natural. The old timer talking to me 40 years ago, told me to give it a reasonable try. That is another reason you need a shorter drive to deliver max force to the ball. When you hang your pinkie over the edge, you are technically adding an inch or so to the club.Just draw back like a tight spring and drive full force into the ball.

Quick Review

1. Get 2 old clubs one driver, one regular.

2. Securely fasten 1 to 2 pounds around the 2 clubs.

3. Swing the clubs regularly. Over, under, sideways and which ever way you can to build up your swing muscles. Swing like you're about to tee off.

4. Take the regular club and place it against an unmovable object. Strain

for 10 seconds several times daily. Go low, then midway, then overhead to use resistance to build swing muscles. Use extreme caution. Don't overdo it.

5. Look at the "Agreement To Myself' promise as you are working out

to reinforce your self.

6. When doing the "Crusher Techniques," be patient. The technique took years to develop. It will seem so strange at first so keep doing it. Practice, practice.

7. Keep exercising your fingers by bending, stretching, rolling, and flexing to help keep fluid from building up in joints.

8. Always check with your Doctor before starting any exercise program.

9. Picture the bottom 1/3 of the ball in your mind's eye. Put an "X" on the imaginary spot.

10. Balled up elastic can be great energy, so be careful. It can fly off and hurt you. Wrap securely. Make it 'A inch high. If you need extra, any department store has it. Just cut it off in 24 inch sections and secure one way on end. Then wrap.

11. Getting a good feel is important. Rock the elastic club handle in your hands to feel that energy. Once you learn to harness that energy, you will see fantastic results.

12. Swing the weighted club with one hand if possible to greatly strengthen swing muscles.

13. One hour of meditation is worth 100 hours of practice. In a very deep relaxed state, while sitting in your easy chair, see yourself hitting those 400 yard golf shots. See yourself winning!

Practice Bonus

The old "Sock Ball" — Roll up a piece of material the size of a golf ball and put rubber bands around it securely. This gives you practice in a confined space. You will get a more solid hit than with, say, a ping pong ball. If you can hit a sock ball solid then you have something going.

www.ingramcontent.com/pod-product-compliance
Lightning Source LLC
LaVergne TN
LVHW011431080426
835512LV00005B/383